Pa's Pearls

Lessons of Lifetime for My Grandkids

John C. Oberheu

*The hardest lessons...
are the best remembered!*

John C. Oberheu

2006

All rights reserved.

Copyright ©2006 by John Oberheu

ISBN: 0-9787995-4-2

Jacket Design by Jennifer Wehrmann

Published and distributed by:
High-Pitched Hum Publishing
321 15th Street North
Jacksonville Beach, FL 32250

www.highpitchedhum.net

No part of this book may be reproduced or transmitted in any form or means, electronic or mechanical, including photocopying, recording, or by any information storage and retrieval system, without permission in writing from the publisher.

Pa's Pearl's

For my loving wife Lucy

. . . the one who encourages and supports my writing habits in so many ways. For enduring my hours at the computer, guarding my seclusion, running endless errands, serving as my "purchase agent," surprising me with welcome refreshments and reminding me of my schedules when I lose track of time.

John C. Oberheu

Pa's Pearl's

CONTENTS

Introduction vii
Dear Nicole, Laura, and Shannon, ... 1
Lesson 1: Burnish Your Escutcheon 3
Lesson 2: Practice Praise Power 9
Lesson 3: Remember Your Smile 13
Lesson 4: Embrace Frugal Instincts 17
Lesson 5: Enhance Your Chance 25
Lesson 6: Honor Hard Work 31
Lesson 7: Escape the Mistake 37
Lesson 8: Talk to Strangers 45
Lesson 9: Don't Buy a Chicago Watch 51
Lesson 10: Focus On the Donut 55
Lesson 11. Use It or Lose It 61
Lesson 12: Mind Your Money 67
Lesson 13: Be A Role Model 83
Epilogue 89

John C. Oberheu

Pa's Pearl's

Introduction

The twelve essays included in this book were originally written as letters to my three granddaughters. At the time they were written and mailed, all three granddaughters were in their teens—the two oldest in college—and all of them preparing for the day they would leave home to begin making their own way in life. It occurred to me that these same truths could be of interest and value to other maturing youth, so I have modified the letters to make them into the essays contained in this book.

John C. Oberheu

Pa's Pearls

Lessons of Lifetime for My Grandkids

Dear Nicole, Laura, and Shannon,

Like most people who have reached my age, I can now look back on a long life and ponder the paths I have taken. I recall good times and bad, hardships and pleasures, joys and sorrows. I take satisfaction from some of the things I did well, but I also have regret for some of my mistakes and missed opportunities. I have often heard friends say, "I wish I had known as a kid what I know now." An old German proverb says, "We get too soon old and too late smart."

There are valuable truths I have learned during my life that I want to pass on to you. They are perspectives gained through a life of many different experiences, with many different teachers. It is my hope that they will give you a head start on some of the lessons that life will likely deal to you.

A bright young executive replacing a CEO who had successfully led a large corporation for twenty years asked him the secret of his success. "Two words," the retiring CEO answered. "Right decisions."

After briefly reflecting about this, the new CEO asked, "And how did you learn to make those right decisions?"

"Two words," the older man answered. "Wrong decisions."

Some of the best-learned lessons in my life came from making wrong decisions. You may have already found that a bad experience can be a very tough teacher, and its lesson can cause pain, embarrassment, or unneeded expense. We usually learn such lessons well, however, and if we are smart, we never forget them. I hope you can learn from some of the bad experiences that have been my teacher.

There are also valuable truths I learned from making good decisions. I have taken several months to write this series of essays that will give you both perspectives. I hope you will read them thoughtfully and perhaps put them away in a safe place for future reference. It is my prayer that the messages they convey will be useful in your life.

With my most sincere love,

Pa

Lesson 1: Burnish Your Escutcheon

Our Regional Director had an amazing command of words. He delighted in using words or phrases that would send us scurrying to our dictionaries. One of my favorites was *escutcheon.*

When I looked up the word I learned that our boss was admonishing us to do our work in a way that would bring respect for our agency. The dictionary defines it as, "a shield on which a coat of arms is presented; a symbol of one's honor or reputation." He wanted us to *burnish* our reputation, or shine it up and keep it bright. The Marine Hymn says it another way: "First to . . . keep our honor clean." I never forgot that word or the meaning it conveyed.

A reputation is something that must be built over a period of time. It is *earned!* It represents the standing that one holds in the opinion of others. Reputations are gradually built through the traits you consistently display by the way you live. Reputations can be either good or bad. You burnish a *good* one by consistently improving and reinforcing desirable traits like the ones below.

Honesty is truthfulness in principles, intentions, words and actions. Honesty will show in small matters as well as important ones. It is apparent in how you respond when the cash register clerk gives you too much change or when you give your child food from the shelves while shopping and then fail to pay for it. It is tested when the checker fails to charge you for one of your purchases or when an incorrect price is tallied. It is very obvious when you cheat on your income tax, shoplift, lie on your expense account, or even when you illegally use a handicap parking space.

Dishonesty shows when an employee takes office supplies home for his child's school use. It shows if one cheats on a test, lies on a job application, or claims credit for something he did not really do.

Truthfulness must consistently show, even in seemingly insignificant matters, and even when it hurts. Each time one is discovered telling a "little white lie" to cover up a mistake or give someone a false impression, it reveals that person's character. It destroys trust and teaches a bad lesson to children who might be watching or listening. If you have a reputation for lying, how will anyone know when you are really telling the truth?

During my working career I had to visit many different wildlife refuges to do periodic inspections. I always tried to spend a little time with each employee at the station to assure myself that there were no personnel problems or irregularities. I was disappointed more than once to learn of refuge managers doing things their workers knew were wrong. They had stolen lumber, made unauthorized use of Government vehicles or equipment, hunted behind closed gates, falsified reports, or practiced other dishonesties. Bosses who can not be trusted in small matters lose the respect of their employees. They also lose the trust of their own bosses. When they are deceitful in small things, it signals they are likely to be the same in more important matters.

Integrity is defined as soundness of moral principle and character. One who has integrity is trustworthy. Integrity shows when one tells the truth even if it hurts, or when a genuine effort is made to locate the owner of something valuable that is found. It is evident when a parent supports the teacher who has taken proper steps to correct a child who misbehaved. It can be seen in the employee who works just as diligently when his boss is gone as he does when the boss is watching.

One of my lifetime heroes is Wayne Wiggins, the North Carolina Refuge Manager who worked for me early in my career. A homespun woodsman who never graduated from high school, Wayne displayed the highest integrity. He had an unusual gift of good common sense, and was held in high respect by the public, as well as the four refuge managers who worked for him.

One night while patrolling in the forest for illegal deer hunting, Wayne chanced upon his own son spotlighting deer. Without a second thought, he arrested him, placed him in handcuffs, and took him to jail. The next day the newspapers carried the front-page story for all to see. Wayne Wiggins was embarrassed, but he had demonstrated integrity. His eight other children had an example they never forgot.

Integrity is evident when one treats bosses, fellow employees or subordinates with consistent fairness and respect. It is undermined by favoritism, discrimination or sexual harassment in any form. It is revealed in all kinds of business or interpersonal dealings.

Reliability is a third ingredient needed for building a good reputation. It can be established only through consistent behavior that leaves a clear trail of conscientious attitude, attention to detail, promptness, fairness, and honesty. Reliable people always keep their word. They believe a promise made is a debt unpaid. They give an employer a day's work for a day's pay. They consistently arrive on time, begin working without being told, and perform their jobs to the best of their ability.

They can be counted on to always do the right thing.

Sensitivity is another important trait found in people with good reputations. Sensitive people recognize unspoken feelings of those around them. Facial expressions or other body language can signal happiness, delight, pleasure, depression, pain, sorrow, disappointment, hurt, loneliness, or anger. A sensitive person tries to respond to such signals in a positive way. An insensitive person is oblivious to others' feelings, and doesn't care about them.

Think of the people in your life who you really admire. They are your role models. They will surely have most if not all of these traits. Remember that you too are a role model for your friends, your children, and others who know you. Building and burnishing your reputation is a lifelong process. The brightness of your escutcheon is easily tarnished when you compromise honesty, integrity, reliability, or sensitivity, even in seemingly trivial ways. Once tarnished, repair can be a very slow and difficult process.

Burnish your escutcheon! It's good for business, for your career, for your friendships; and it's a good example for those who see you as a role model. It's a good motto for your life!

Lesson 2: Practice Praise Power

It was Smitty's last meeting with his supervisor and peers—and only days before he retired. His boss congratulated him on a successful career, read the words of a Commendable Service Award, and presented him with the usual retirement plaque.

The meeting continued with other business when, suddenly, without any explanation, Smitty rose to his feet and hurried out of the room. After this brief interruption, the meeting resumed. About ten minutes later he returned.

After the meeting I cornered him to ask if he had been ill. He shook his head. Then he answered softly, "I was reading the award. It's . . . it's the first time anyone ever said anything good about my work, and I . . . I just kind of lost it."

Our Personnel Management Office had contacted my boss several weeks earlier to suggest we might want to prepare the customary Commendable Service Award for his retirement. This meeting of our scattered field staff was an opportunity for presenting it. I had written a short commendation summarizing his career and telling about the many people he had helped. It was pretty much a retirement "attaboy," not an award for unusual or outstanding performance. To him, however, it was recognition he had craved for over forty years, a boss telling him that he did good work.

This incident made a deep impression on me, one I resolved to always remember as I progressed in my career and moved up to supervisory and management positions: *Recognize and compliment a good job when you see it. Don't wait for a retirement ceremony.*

It's very easy to get caught up in the urgency of daily routines and problem solving and to overlook the good work of those who always excel and never cause trouble. I'm sure you have experienced a warm glow of satisfaction when you are complimented on something you have done well. Everybody likes recognition. Good managers know it is a strong motivator, even for those who never try and don't care. It's a proven Dale Carnegie principle: "Give encouragement and motivation by focusing on the things people do right. Overlook failures, or handle them very gingerly." Try to find something, anything, that even the poorest employee does well, and praise it. It can bring surprising results.

I found that praise works well not only in management, but in all kinds of interpersonal relationships. It can make a friend out of someone who dislikes you, cheer up someone who is

Pa's Pearl's

depressed, or bring hope to someone discouraged. Friends, neighbors, bosses, subordinates, your doctor, a store clerk, your yard guy, your trash man, even strangers; all will respond to a compliment if it is truthful and sincere. It can make a person's day when someone just notices and tells them. Important to remember, however, is that whatever you say must be truthful, not exaggerated, obviously untrue, or intentionally flattering, or your motive will be suspect.

In my twelve years as a school volunteer, I have helped more than 250 first graders learn to read. I found that they also respond to compliments on things they do well. I could tell the difference while they were reading. When I praised them for figuring out a tough word, or remembering something we had just learned, it seemed to give them a push to try harder. I began using praise with every one of them, frequently and consistently. They never tire of it. Every child, even the slowest one, does something well that can be the subject for praise. The motivation it gives can spill over to bring improvement, even for other things they have not done well.

Most of us know the feelings of regret we can have when someone close to us is suddenly taken by sickness or accident. We wish we had told them how much we noticed, admired, and appreciated the things they did! Don't wait until it's too late! It's a good thought to fix permanently in our minds: *Watch for things that people do well and tell them about it—on the spot!*

Lesson 3: Remember Your Smile

I was crossing the street during the noonday rush when I glimpsed a pretty face approaching me. As we passed, our eyes met and she flashed the warmest, friendliest smile I had ever seen. She was gone in an instant, but the impression of that smile would not go away. At home that evening I wanted to write about it. I sat down and penned a letter to the newspaper editor. Then I thought, "Nobody will care about how a pretty girl's smile affected me," and I threw it in the wastebasket.

That was twenty-five years ago, but I can still see her smile. I can no longer picture her face, but the smile is indelible. I have never before tried to explain why it affected me as it did. I think it conveyed friendliness and worth. It said, "You are important, and I could be your friend." I guess it impressed me so much because her smile was so warm and real.

The author Dale Carnegie in his classic book *How to Win Friends and Influence People* recognizes the power of a smile. Students in his training course are asked to practice smiling at people and report the results at the next class. When I tried it I was amazed. Riding the commuter train to work each morning, I would see crowds of faces, each one immersed in his or her own thoughts. Some read, some slept, and some stared at the commercials posted on the overhead panels. Not a smile in a trainload, and not easy to even catch someone's eye.

When I could catch a person's eye I flashed a smile and almost always got one in return. I tried to make smiles a part of my regular routine. Often this unspoken communication was enough to open an informal friendship. Faces that had been familiar but usually preoccupied or businesslike suddenly became ones that recognized me and smiled. We would smile every time we met, and then it became easy to start a conversation. They became a part of my "train family."

I liked the challenge of bringing a smile to a glum face. One of my favorites was the matronly lady who operated the elevator in my Washington, DC office building. I don't know what life had dealt her, but she always had the most sad and dour look as she mechanically operated the elevator, never looking at the faces of those who rode with her. I began making a point of standing next to her, smiling and speaking to her every morning. I watched a remarkable change. She would break into a smile the instant she saw me, and we always had something to talk about in the brief rides to my office floor. This lady, who must

Pa's Pearl's

have had a lonely, difficult life, became my friend and always helped brighten my day.

When we moved to a new city with toll bridges, the collectors wore faces that were bored and detached. I liked giving them a smile and cheerful greeting to see if I could get one in return. I remember one toll collector who was the exception. A white-haired, older lady, she greeted all who passed with her own lively, friendly smile and cheerful greeting. She made the commuters smile. What a refreshing difference!

Then there was Bailey. He played and sang at a piano bar where my wife and I liked to go on Saturday nights. He knew almost every song you could think of and always had a nice line of chatter and humor. I was impressed by the framed motto he kept on his piano: "If you see someone without a smile, give him one of yours." He practiced his motto with his own big smile, and he spread good cheer and happiness to everyone who came to enjoy his music.

Julia Roberts has been said to be the world's most famous movie star. Her picture has been plastered on the cover of almost every glamour magazine, and every time she makes a move, the entire world knows about it. As I watched her movie "Notting Hill," it struck me—her electric beauty and engaging personality come from her smile! With a straight, solemn face she is pretty, but when she breaks into even a slight smile, her real attractiveness begins to show. And when she really beams her warmest, friendliest, happiest smile, you are completely captured by it. You love her!

A New York department store posted this reminder during the Christmas rush:

"The Value of a Smile: It costs nothing, but creates much. It enriches those who receive without impoverishing those who give. It happens in a flash, but the memory of it can last a lifetime. It is of no earthly good to anyone until it is given away. Nobody needs a smile so much as those who have none left to give."

It's really true! There's *magic* in a smile! When I see an extra-friendly one, I always think about the pretty girl who passed that magic to me. Her memory will never fade, and I sometimes think to myself, "I wonder where she is today. She could have been another Julia Roberts."

Lesson 4: Embrace Frugal Instincts

My wife and I were at a cookout that was our sendoff for a promotion and move to Washington, DC. When I unwrapped a gift from my co-workers, I found a framed picture painted by our illustrator to commemorate the occasion. There I was with my carpool riders, driving a stripped-down version of my red Chevy II station wagon. In back of the passenger's seat was a stack of moneybags overflowing with gold coins. On the side of the worn and tattered vehicle a motto was inscribed: "Frugal Is a Nice Word."

I had been driving my station wagon for ten years, and it had over 100,000 miles. My carpool members and fellow workers used to constantly kid me about my "vintage" car, and about being so "tight" that I carried my own lunch to work and even recycled my used lunch bags. It was all good-natured kidding, of course, and it never bothered me. In fact, I was proud of being thrifty, and I liked the motto painted on the side of the cartoon car. It fit me.

The dictionary defines frugal as, "Characterized by thriftiness and avoidance of waste." The word thrift is defined as "The sensible and cautious management of money and goods in order to waste as little as possible and obtain maximum value." I try to practice both.

I was born during the latter years of the Great Depression. My parents *had* to be frugal to survive. We were a family of seven children, and all nine of us lived on my father's meager salary as a missionary in India. My mother was an expert at stretching Pop's income to cover all our needs. To this day, I wonder how she ever did it. Rent, food, clothes, shoes, doctor, dentist, all of our bills. She balanced the family income and expenses without ever buying things on credit. If she couldn't pay for something, she wouldn't buy it until she could.

I grew up with a healthy respect for thrift. Mom frequently quoted Ben Franklin's old proverb, "A penny saved is a penny earned." She found all kinds of ways to cut corners and save, and taught us to put money away for a "rainy day." During World War II my brothers and I saved money from selling scrap iron, doing chores for the neighbors, and from the modest allowance our oldest sister gave us from her paycheck. We invested regularly in ten-cent War Stamps that were pasted one by one in a stamp book that could be traded for a $25 War Bond when it was filled.

Back in the U.S.A., we learned how to do all the minor maintenance and repair jobs around our

Pa's Pearl's

home. We helped Pop in the vegetable garden and helped Mom can fruit and vegetables. Mom bought a hair clipper and I learned to give haircuts to my younger brothers. When I got good enough, I also cut Pop's hair. We learned how to change the oil in the car, how to do our own plumbing repairs, and how to refinish floors. I built furniture for our home: a kitchen cabinet, a clothes cabinet, stools, bedside tables, and even a regular office desk with seven drawers for Dad's office. They were not "store-bought," but they served our purpose.

"Waste not, want not" was a motto that both my wife and I learned in our own families. We never throw away food left over from a meal. We always shop for bargains, and never waste money on buying prestige-label clothes. We wore hand-me-down clothes a lot, and even though I had no older brothers, I was always happy to get "new" hand-me-downs from our friends. My first new suit was my oldest sister's gift to me when I graduated from college. We always owned cars that got the best gas mileage and had the least maintenance costs, and were not ashamed to drive them until they were worn out.

These principles of thrift learned while we were "poor folks" have served me well. There were hard times during our fifty years of marriage when we had to drastically cut expenses to make ends meet. We never, however, lacked for anything we needed, and we never spent more than our income. With the exception of home and car loans, we never went in debt. Through all our years together, we were always able to put something away for the future.

That brings me to another important principle of thrift: *Always pay yourself first.* Put some of your earnings away for a future need—a college education, a new television set, an unforeseen emergency, or, most important of all, a secure retirement income. We arranged automatic deductions from our checking account to go to the credit union for car payments. When the loan was paid off, we didn't buy a new car. We kept driving our debt-free car, and kept the payments going into college funds for our daughters. When daughter Teri was ready to go off to college, we were driving a ten-year-old car but were ready to pay for her education.

When IRAs became available as a way to save for retirement, we began putting away the maximum allowable amount. The money invested in the IRAs was not taxable, and we saved the twenty-eight percent of it that would have gone for income tax. Now that I am no longer working, we receive monthly payments from my IRA that will

Pa's Pearl's

continue to supplement our pensions for the rest of our lives.

The Social Security Retirement System of today is not designed to pay a retirement income that is adequate for living expenses. The minimum age for retirement payments to begin has been raised, future payments are likely to be reduced, and the very future of the System is in question. A prudent person will not rely solely on Social Security for retirement income, but will make provisions for other income through instruments like IRAs and 401-Ks. The earlier you start such savings plans, the more the "magic of compounding" can work to build your nest egg.

Some employers provide a retirement plan in which they will match the retirement contributions of employees. It is a wise retirement strategy to always contribute the full amount that will maximize the match received from your employer. It's a no-brainer to take full advantage of this freebie. Think of your retirement contribution as a bill you must pay regularly.

If you inherit money or get a salary bonus, you may suddenly have enough money to buy some luxury item you really don't need. Resist the temptation until you have carefully thought about it. Try to defer your gratification. Might not this money, properly invested, make your retirement days less difficult? Never buy something just because you have the money to do it. Though you might be able to buy it, you might not be able to afford it.

Over sixty years have passed since the worst days of the Great Depression. Most of those living today never had to deal with the severe unemployment and poverty of that time. Low-income people nowadays have the benefit of unemployment compensation, food stamps, welfare payments, and Medicaid. Very few understand how far a really frugal life style can stretch a meager income during times of hardship. Without such an understanding, they often make spending choices that lead them deeper and deeper into debt, until their only choice is bankruptcy. Too many times this is followed by a repeated pattern of the same financial mistakes.

There are infinite ways to stretch a budget so that income covers *necessary* expenses. You can drive a small used car instead of a hot new one, turn lights out when you leave a room, set your thermostat lower in the winter and wear a sweater, cook thrifty meals at home instead of eating out, buy clothes at a Goodwill Store, ride a bus to work and carry your own lunch, walk or ride a bike to the drugstore, drink water instead of Coke . . . and on and on. One enterprising lady started her own newspaper called *The Penny Pincher* that gave endless ways for saving money and paid readers for sending in their ideas. You can easily think of your own ways to cut costs by just being truthful with yourself about what you *really* need.

Most young people of today are fortunate to have lived in a family that has not had to practice the difficult principles of thrift. If they are fortunate, this will continue in their future. But in almost every life, unexpected calamities happen which can create a financial crisis. Perhaps a spouse dies, a home is destroyed by storm or fire, or a job is lost. Should it ever happen to you, don't despair. You can survive. I hope you will remember this essay, and that it will give you the courage and resolve you need.

In summary, these are the life lessons I learned about the values of being frugal:

A penny saved is a penny earned. Every time you find a way to cut the cost of something you need, you increase the amount of discretionary income you can allot to other needs.

Pay yourself first. Begin a systematic savings plan. Now!

Remember future needs and defer your gratification. It is human nature to want more than you can afford, but "wants" are not the same as "needs," and you must learn the difference.

Never be ashamed of making a thrifty choice on how you live. Take pride in living your life in a way that gives you independence and self-sufficiency.

And don't forget my motto, "Frugal is a nice word!"

Lesson 5: Enhance Your Chance

"A fool and his money are soon parted."

My mother was smiling as she recalled and quoted an old Chinese proverb she had learned many years before. She had listened sympathetically to my tale of woe, and it was her way of telling me I had just learned a valuable lesson in life.

It all started one evening long ago when my date and I went to a rural county fair with a group of high school friends. Like most fairs, it had contests for best live stock, best vegetables, best pies, and many others. It also had the usual carnival midway with various rides, sideshows, shooting galleries, tests of strength or skill, and other amusements.

As we strolled hand in hand among the many booths, we came to one where the operator challenged me to win a huge teddy bear for my date. It was a beautiful, huggable teddy bear, so we paused to see how the game was played. The operator would place ten ping-pong balls in a cradle that released them to roll down a short ramp where they randomly came to rest in one of thirty or forty holes on a flat deck. Each hole was inscribed with a number value of zero to nine. He would add up the total of the ten numbers for the occupied holes, and then refer to a posted chart of various totals to find the point value. A total score of ten points would win the teddy bear.

Since my date really admired the teddy bear, I thought it was worth several tries at twenty-five cents each. On the first roll he quickly added up the total and gave me five points. Wow! Half way there! The next time I won two more points. I was well on my way toward winning, so I kept investing in one more roll. I earned several half points and finally reached a total of eight points.

When my winning streak slowed down, I started adding up my own totals to make sure he was being honest. I had never intended to spend so much at one booth, so after a few more tries, we started to leave. He stopped me by adding a $20 bill to the prize, but raising the cost to fifty cents a roll. This changed the cost/benefit ratio for more tries, so I rolled a few more. I added another half point but was running low on cash so started to leave again.

Again he stopped me. "Look here," he said. "You are so close to winning, I'm going to give you this portable radio with the $20 and the teddy bear." It was a beautiful, red radio worth $30 or more. I knew I could win it if I just kept trying.

My date watched quietly offering no advice.

This time he raised the cost to a dollar per roll. I thought I still had enough money to win and kept trying until I was flat broke. Now I was on a date that had just started and had no money to spend for the rest of the evening. How embarrassing! I found my brother who had been more careful with his cash and floated a loan. I was able to salvage part of the evening, but we could not enjoy as many things as I had planned. And for me, losing all that money was not my idea of a good time.

Later that night I figured out what had happened. He gave me all of the early points just to get me hooked. I didn't realize it, because I had not bothered to check his addition. Only specified totals had any point value, and I doubt that any of the possible totals would give five points. The game was rigged with very little or no chance for him to lose—or for me to win.

Without the big head start on points I would never have played the game as long as I did. He had played me like a fine violin, keeping me in the game by adding tantalizing rewards just out of reach, but decreasing his own risk by raising the costs. He was a con man with an expert understanding of human nature.

It was a classic lesson in my "school of hard

knocks," a bad experience I would never forget. I didn't like thinking of myself as a fool, but had to agree I had acted like one. I should have recognized that game as one of pure chance, not one that tested strength, wits, skill, or endurance. Games of chance are always rigged in favor of the management so they can be profitable. An unprofitable business doesn't last long.

Gambling casinos are a good example. The lavish buildings, glitzy signs, bright lights, and extravagant furnishings are all proof they are not losing money. The low cost tours, inexpensive meals, and free drinks are all bait to induce patrons to lose enough money to make their business profitable.

I never made that mistake again. Other than the few single lottery tickets I've bought through the years, it was the last time I ever played a game of chance for something of value. The way I see it, why play a game where your chances of winning are controlled in such a way that most players lose? Casinos are nothing more than a place for people to throw their money away for amusement. If one gambles long enough, total winnings will always be a small fraction of total losses.

Lotteries are another easy way to throw away money. If you pause to consider your odds of winning, you know your tickets buy you only a

Pa's Pearl's

dream of what you would do if you actually won. Think about how many people have to lose to pay for one person to win a million dollars.

I hope you will always remember what I learned from a difficult lesson of my life: *Enhance your chance—don't take one that is not in your favor!*

Lesson 6: Honor Hard Work

The trash truck pulls to a hard stop in front of my driveway. Two men, riding on the small platforms at each corner of its rear, step lightly to the street and hurry to waiting trash barrels and bulging bags on either side of the street. They deftly carry and dump trash into the maw of the big truck, return empty barrels to their owner's driveway, and hurry to the next house where the truck has already stopped, waiting for them to repeat the process.

I know of no one in our society who works harder than the men who provide our trash service. They go all day at this pace, from one pickup point to the next, emptying barrel after heavy barrel of trash into their trucks. They lift, carry, and dump tons of trash each day. They must have muscles of iron and amazing endurance to keep this up all day. I have seen them in the late afternoon working with the same vigor and efficiency as in the morning, regardless of weather conditions. They also work on holidays.

I think they must have ravenous appetites when their day is done and they sit down to their evening meal. Surely sleep comes quickly as their tired bodies are restored for their next active day.

John C. Oberheu

The way they do their job, they must take personal pride in it. I understand they are very well paid, and I believe they well deserve it.

Not many jobs could be less esteemed than spending entire days lifting and disposing of other people's wastes. Most people probably look at the trash man's job as menial and undignified, certainly a job for someone who can't find anything better. But if you haven't guessed by now, I have great admiration for these men, and for others like them who hard work every day.

Many people around us work faithfully at tasks we would never consider doing. A lot of us tend to completely ignore them as we go about our much more "important" activities. Think about those who clean public toilets, sweep and polish floors, clean litter from our highways, clean out sewers, drive delivery trucks, repair streets and build homes. Picture the migrant workers who harvest our crops, or dig with shovels to bury TV cable; the dish washer or fast-order cook at a small café; those who work all night, begin work very early or work long hours. All of them are performing very demanding, low-prestige jobs. *But, they are working!*

Not only are they working and making their own ways in our society, they are providing us with necessary services we need for our way of life.

Pa's Pearl's

They are usually not well paid but are staying off welfare roles. Theirs may not be glamorous or glorious work, but it is important and honest. The people who do it deserve our respect and gratitude, and we should never look down on them. After all, they are working for *our* benefit!

I learned respect for hard labor during the summer months of my high school years when I worked on farms near our rural town. Most farm duties are very physical, but some of the hardest days I remember were with the wheat threshing crews. Bundles of wheat grain had to be loaded on wagons from shocks in the fields and taken to the threshing machine for separating the grain from the straw. Each 12-inch diameter bundle of wheat stalks, still heavy with their grain, had to be loaded on a wagon, stacked by the wagon driver, taken to the thresher, and unloaded into the machine. Heavy bags of grain had to be filled, loaded onto wagons, and hauled to the barn.

I worked 12-hour days on each of the various threshing crew jobs. Throwing those 25-pound bundles on the wagon with a pitchfork, one at a time, all day long, was the hardest of all. I wanted to try it, but the farmer I worked for didn't think I could do it. I was a skinny kid, and it took a person with strong arms and back. He agreed to give me a try, but doubted I could last all day. As that long day wore on, it got tougher and tougher, but I was determined to last it out. That night at the dinner table, the farmer bragged on how well I had done. When I collapsed in bed I knew I would wake up with sore muscles, but I was proud of doing the day's work of a real man.

Since that day, I have done many kinds of hard labor such as loading and unloading all our furniture and possessions on a rented moving truck, manually digging a long ditch with a shovel, building fences, cutting and splitting firewood, clearing dense brush with hand tools, etc. That day on the threshing crew, however, stands out in my memory. It taught me that my body was very capable of doing hard physical labor, and that it can be very satisfying.

I get a special satisfaction from doing hard work. It's a feeling of accomplishment, a feeling that I have taken on a difficult challenge and conquered it. It gives me peace of mind knowing a tough and perhaps distasteful task is done. Enjoying the luxury of a hot shower after a day of hard labor, I feel a warm sensation of well being as tired muscles release endorphins into my blood stream. When you yourself perform hard work, you can truly appreciate those who do it all the time.

Yes, I have great admiration for people who do

menial jobs and just plain old hard work. They need to know they are appreciated. I like to speak to them when I get a chance, so they know I respect what they do. I like to know the names of those I see regularly, like the custodian at the public school where I volunteer, the waitresses at the restaurants where I eat, or the ones who do my yard work. They become my friends, and they know I appreciate the work they do. I like to remember the trash crews and our mail carrier at Christmas, and I like to give generous tips to those who serve our food at restaurants. Everyone likes to be appreciated for a job well done.

I hope sharing my thoughts about the importance of hard work and the self-satisfaction it can give will help you gain a new appreciation for their importance. I trust that my perspectives of the people who work hard for us will remind you of the respect they deserve and how their friendship can enrich our lives as well as theirs.

Lesson 7: Escape the Mistake

It had to be one of the dumbest things I ever did, but it took me thirteen years to figure it out! It was the day I lit my first cigarette.

My family has a history of smokers. My grandfather smoked uncured burley tobacco in a smelly old pipe until the day he died. My dad smoked from as far back as I can remember until the day of his massive stroke. As a kid, I didn't see anything wrong with it. My Mom always fussed about his smoking, but she could never get him to quit. She hated the smell of smoke and ashtrays and wouldn't allow smoking at the dinner table. But in those days, smoking was not considered harmful. Nobody talked about the dangers of smoking, and there were no studies showing that it was unhealthy.

I guess it was inevitable that I would one day start myself. My best friend and I first tried smoking when we were high school seniors. On our way to see a movie, we bought a pack, smoked several during the evening, and then hid them for future use under a rural bridge on our way home. When I went away to college I had the freedom to smoke any time I wanted, and I quickly developed a habit. I liked smoking. It gave me a grown-up, independent feeling.

Smoking became a social thing. In a circle of friends, we would all light up and enjoy smoking like those we considered stylish and modern. Most of the movie stars smoked, and I used to study how they lit up, held their cigarettes, and blew their smoke. At first I hid it from my mother, but she was able to smell it on me. Gradually she quit fussing about it, and I even smoked in our home. Cigarettes were cheap at only twenty-five cents a pack and less than $2.00 a carton.

I was hooked. I smoked after every meal; I smoked when I was studying hard; I smoked whenever I was under any stress; and I got the urge to smoke every time I was near someone who lit up. It was the last thing I did before going to bed.

At college, I learned to smoke a pipe and enjoyed the fragrant smell of special tobaccos. Later in life, when I could afford it, I liked cigars. I smoked in closed cars which also held suffering non-smokers. I sat in closed-door meetings where the entire room was clouded in smoke. Twenty or more years ago, smokers were in the majority, and they were not considerate of non-smokers. To show how much I loved smoking I would knock ashes from my cigarette into my coffee and then drink it.

Pa's Pearl's

In 1963, some forty-three years ago, the Surgeon General published the first public warning about the dangers of smoking. This confirmed my growing feeling that I shouldn't be doing it. I had a continuous smoker's cough and could tell that I was too quickly out of breath during any kind of exercise.

I'm proud to tell you that I took the Surgeon General's warning to heart. I threw out my pipe and cigarettes and never smoked again. Let me assure you, it was not easy. I had the deep craving for tobacco hundreds of times a day. Every time I saw anyone light up I wanted one for myself. I had my worst craving right after a meal. It was hard to enjoy a cocktail party without lighting up like so many of the others. When the craving was really bad, I chewed tobacco or used snuff to ease the feeling. I chewed gum by the pack—until my jaws were tired and sore. It took about a year for the craving to finally go away, but it took three years before I could watch someone light up without wanting to smoke.

Today I am probably more sensitive to smoke than someone who never smoked. The smallest trace of smoke in a room irritates my lungs and makes me cough. I can pass someone in a hallway and know from the smell that he is a heavy smoker. My wife smoked for over forty-three years, and though she often tried, was never able to quit until she needed major surgery to replace part of her aorta. Doctors told her smoking helped cause it to become so clogged that it could no longer carry blood to her legs.

Today everyone knows that smoking is bad for you. Smokers who care about their health are either quitting or trying to quit. Many who really want to quit can't seem to do it. Make no mistake! Smoking is addictive, and smoking will own you. The best way to keep out of its clutches is to never even try it.

I asked my life insurance agent how much time a kid who started smoking at age eighteen would cut off his life. He looked up the statistics and told me—six years! If you begin smoking at eighteen, and live as long as the average smoker who starts at that age, you will live only fifty-five more years while non-smokers will live another sixty-one years. You will have given up one day of your life for every nine days that you smoked Now you may know smokers who lived a lot longer than seventy-three years (that's eighteen plus fifty-five), but, remember, for every one of those there is another who died younger than age seventy-three.

Anyone smoking at age forty-five or older is part of a group that is dying twice as fast as non-smokers! That's why life insurance companies must charge smokers more for their insurance. They would soon go bankrupt if they did not. There is no doubting these statistics.

Below are many good reasons why you should never try even one cigarette:

Smokers shorten their own lives. Smoking is a primary cause of heart and lung diseases and contributes to many other health problems such as cancer, heart attacks, strokes, ulcers, chronic bronchitis, and emphysema. Smoking kills more Americans each year than died in battle during World War II and the Vietnam War combined. Every day, more than 1,200 Americans die from smoking-related causes, the equivalent of three or four fully loaded jumbo jets crashing with no survivors.

Smokers affect other people's lives. A recent Harvard University study showed that regular exposure to second-hand smoke doubles the risk of heart disease. Federal, state, and city governments have recognized this and restricted smoking in offices, restaurants, and other public places. Why should helpless children or non-smokers who care about their own health have to breathe smoke from those who don't care?

Smoking during pregnancy causes birth defects. Some mothers find it impossible to stop smoking even when they are pregnant and when they know it is harming their baby. Think about that! Do you really want to start a bad habit you may never be able to stop?

Smokers smell like tobacco smoke. It's a fact that every non-smoker knows. Smoke hangs in their clothes, in their hair, and on their skin. Smoker's breath is strong and repulsive to non-smokers, but smokers themselves can't smell it.

Smoking is no longer cool. The habit is repugnant to those who don't smoke, and most people are now non-smokers. Smokers must go like outcasts to smoking zones away from their work to indulge their habit.

Smoking can affect your employment. Workers who smoke waste time because they must leave their work to have a cigarette. Employers are finding that smokers take more sick days and that their health insurance costs are greater. Some employers will not hire a person who smokes even if it is only when they are away from their workplace.

Smoking is expensive. A pack of cigarettes costs $2.50 to $3.00. If you smoke a pack a day, that is about $1,000 a year! Aren't there better things to do with your cash?

Smoking is an unnatural act. It draws waste products from burning leaves deep into lungs that are naturally irritated by anything other than clean air. The first time anyone inhales smoke, he or she will cough violently. Smoking causes high blood pressure by constricting arteries, and it makes poisonous carbon monoxide displace needed oxygen in the blood. That's why smokers tire so easily.

I know what it's like to be a smoker, because I have been one. I'll never know how much the thirteen years I smoked might have affected the health of my two daughters, or even my own life span and quality of life. I was able to quit, with a lot of difficulty, but many smokers who really, really want to quit, can't do it.

That's why I feel so strongly about this lesson I learned from my own life. It's why I hate to see young people experiment with a dangerous habit that will change their life. It's why I have stood before fifth grade graduates at Seabreeze Elementary School for the last ten years to give them the facts that are in this essay. Some kids are fortunate to have grown up in a home where neither parent smoked and where they had good role models. But most young people will still face the peer pressure of friends tempting them to try something "adult" and daring. I hope my story can give them the courage and resolve to resist.

The smoking habit is nothing better than slow suicide, a proven way to ruin your health and shorten your life. Don't ever let it trap you!

Lesson 8: Talk to Strangers

Horror stories abound and protective parents pound it into their kids from the earliest age—"Don't talk to strangers!" Child molestation, kidnapping, and Amber Alerts are enough to frighten anyone, so some children grow up fearful of the unfamiliar face. Many of them will not respond to a friendly greeting even when their parents are with them. Some won't even look at you. More than a few grow up with a lasting aversion for speaking to anyone they don't know.

Adults too must learn to be careful for thugs, sexual predators, rapists, purse-snatchers, car hijackers, and other criminals looking for victims on our streets. Stories carried by the news media tell of their crimes and give advice on how to protect ourselves. It's enough to make all of us wary of anyone we don't know.

In the rural areas and small towns where I grew up, we never heard of such problems. As kids, we were taught to respect our elders and politely respond to a friendly greeting. Both my mother and father had outgoing personalities and enjoyed making new friends. But still, just like most kids, I grew up with a natural shyness and reluctance for talking to people I didn't know.

John C. Oberheu

During my college years I hitchhiked sixty miles to and from my home almost every weekend to get my laundry done and enjoy Mom's cooking. Though it would not be a safe thing to do today, I rode with hundreds of strangers from all walks of life. I rode with males and females, rich and poor, black and white, educated and illiterate. When strangers stopped to give me a ride, it was often because they wanted someone to keep them company. Truck drivers needed me to help them stay awake. I made myself speak with them all and soon found that I not only enjoyed it, but I learned from it.

As I matured, I discovered other good reasons to talk with strangers. Anyone you meet can be your teacher. Each has lived in a unique environment and experienced different life styles, adventures, stresses, pleasures, and tragedies. Each one can help increase our knowledge and understanding of the world we live in.

My sister Anita was a person who never knew a stranger. She chatted with everyone she met, people standing in grocery lines, sitting in restaurants or bars, shopping in stores or flea markets, attending ball games or conventions, or riding buses and commuter trains. She had a way of drawing people out of their shell to tell about themselves and the things they knew. She showed me how much fun it could be, and I learned from her.

Wherever we go, there are opportunities to learn from strangers. They can give us directions when we are lost, recommend a good place to eat, describe a new way to prepare fish, suggest a dream vacation, or tell an amusing anecdote. We can learn about other cultures, other life styles, unusual historic events, terrifying life experiences, unbelievable hardships, the misery of poverty, the joy of success, pitfalls of investment, or unusual occupations.

There are millions of interesting facts like this about our world that we will never know. But each time we add something new to our own body of knowledge, our life is enriched, our perspectives are broadened, and our ability to converse with others is expanded.

A hungry homeless man taught me it is unfair to judge people by their clothes. A blind woman I met on a commuter train became a close friend who continues to give me rare insight into her world of disability. A stranger I met at the gym is a postman who explained how the daily mail is sorted and delivered. Another gym acquaintance is an artist who drew a pencil portrait of me which now hangs in our home. An old timer waiting in a long line with me to mail Christmas packages told fascinating stories about growing up in a South Alabama logging camp during the Great Depression.

Busses, trains, airplanes, and taxies are all good places to meet interesting strangers. My older sister Antoinette tells a true story about our grandfather. He was one of the oldest of thirteen children in his family. Riding a train from his home in South Dakota to attend his youngest sister's wedding in Milwaukee, he began a conversation with the young man seated beside him. As they became better acquainted, he discovered they were not only going to the same destination, they were also going to the same wedding! Then to his even greater amazement, he learned he was seated next to his own youngest brother, one he had not seen for years!

Most strangers are open to friendship. They want to belong to a familiar group and be accepted by those around them. Almost everyone has experienced the anxiety and tension of being with a group of total strangers. We know what it's like to go to a party, a new job, a new school, or a new church, hoping to meet someone who will make us feel welcome and more at ease. If we see a person who looks uncomfortable and lonely in such a situation, it's a great opportunity to be helpful and perhaps gain a new friend.

Pa's Pearl's

The Bible carries an interesting message about strangers. Hebrews 13:2 reads, "Do not forget to entertain strangers, for by so doing some people have entertained angels without knowing it."

Yes, we must always be alert for criminals who would do us harm, and sadly, the days of safe hitchhiking with strangers have passed. But it is foolish to shut ourselves off from everyone we don't know. Strangers are all around us, and there are many places where we can safely talk. There are countless things we can learn from them to enrich our lives and expand our experiences. So my advice to you is this: *Remember the principles of personal safety, to be sure, but don't miss an opportunity to learn something new by meeting a stranger!*

Lesson 9: Don't Buy a Chicago Watch

One of the toughest lessons in my "School of Hard Knocks" came during my senior year at college. During spring of that year, my major professor wanted me to go to Chicago to take a competitive test for a job with the Illinois Conservation Department. This trip was pretty scary stuff for me because I didn't know the first thing about getting around in big cities.

As it turned out my roommate Bob had a sister who lived in Chicago, and he had been there enough to know his way around. He offered to go with me and arranged for us to spend a weekend with his sister. It was a real adventure for me. We hitchhiked there, making the 300-mile trip with only two different rides. The second driver dropped us off at a commuter train station with instructions on how to take the elevated train to Bob's sister's home.

After taking the State's test on a Saturday morning, we had time to explore some of the wonders of the big city. I am sure every native there could tell I was from the country from the way I looked at the tall buildings and other sights.

On Sunday we decided not to hitchhike back

to college because we wanted to be sure to arrive there at a reasonable hour. Standing in line to buy tickets at the bus station, a well-dressed young man approached and offered to sell me a beautiful new watch, still in its case. I could see that it was expensive and guessed it was stolen. When I asked where he got it, he gave an evasive answer. I told him I wasn't interested, and he moved on to other people in the bus station.

After buying our tickets, we started off to see a bit more of Chicago before our bus was scheduled to leave. Still thinking about the watch, I told Bob, "You know, there must be a lot of stolen stuff sold in Chicago. A guy might be able to get a real bargain on a good watch."

After a bit more talk, I decided to go back and look at the watch. I had twenty dollars left after buying my ticket, and I thought that might be enough. The man was still in the bus station and I asked to see the watch. Glancing around carefully, he said "Come into the men's room where it's safe."

In the dimly lit restroom he showed it to me in its fancy case. It was a beautiful gold watch with diamonds set in the face at the quarter-hour markers and rubies at the other hour markers. "See," he said. "Water-proof, shock-proof, anti-magnetic, and it has a 23-jewel action."

Pa's Pearl's

Before the days of battery-operated quartz watches, the most accurate, long-lasting, and expensive watches had jeweled bearings. I guessed the watch would have been worth one hundred to one hundred fifty dollars, a very expensive watch in those days. He wanted twenty dollars, but since it was stolen I figured I might get it for even less. I offered him fifteen dollars and he readily agreed. He put the watch on my wrist though I was already wearing my old one. He said it would keep the police from being suspicious.

When Bob saw the watch, he wanted one for himself. He went back and soon returned with one he got for only ten dollars. Walking down the sidewalk admiring our new purchases, my friend made a startling discovery. "You know, these look just like the watches they're selling in the drug store back home," he said. "They're on a cardboard display on the checkout counter and sell for seven dollars and fifty cents!"

Our hearts sank at the thought that our bargain watches might not be real bargains. Too late we realized that the guy might have bought dozens of watches like this at a wholesale price of even less than seven dollars and fifty cents. The gift case doubtless came from a different watch and he was using it over and over.

At home the following weekend my worst

fears were realized. A jeweler friend appraised my watch at seven or eight dollars. It didn't really have a 23-jewel working mechanism, and the diamonds and rubies in its face were only pretty pieces of glass. Within two months it stopped running.

The fifteen dollars I blew on that watch was almost two weeks' wages at the sixty cents an hour I earned on my part-time job. The deal was not, however, a complete loss. I had purchased a classic and unforgettable lesson for my life. *When you do business with a crook, don't expect to be treated fairly.*

I still have my Chicago watch. It has not run even one hour since the day it failed fifty-four years ago. Its "gold" finish is rusting, and the loosened "jewels" in its face rattle under its crystal. It is completely worthless except as a symbol of the valuable lesson it taught me. I can't even guess how many shady "bargain" deals I've refused through the years because I never forgot that mistake. I hope you too can benefit from the hard lesson I learned when I compromised my integrity and dealt with a Chicago crook. *Can the cons! Don't let a con man take you to the cleaners!*

Lesson 10: Focus On the Donut

As a kid of twelve, I was intrigued by the donut machine in the dime store of downtown Paducah, Kentucky. Its stainless steel carousel held about thirty little compartments that rotated within a large pot filled with hot grease. Raw donuts fell one at a time into the compartments and cooked as they circled the pot. As they neared their starting point, a lever lifted them into a chute that took them sliding to a waiting tray for powdered sugar or frosting.

It was fascinating to watch the production of those delicious confections. On the glass that protected viewers from the hot grease was a little ditty. I loved it! It had a rhyme that was easy to remember, and it was a good motto for one's life—a proverb if you will.

> "As you travel down life's road,
> What e'er may be your goal,
> Keep your eye upon the donut,
> And not upon the hole."

Though I never forgot this little poem, I really didn't realize how it could apply to my life until years later when I became a Refuge Supervisor and

John C. Oberheu

District Manager. For self-improvement, I made a practice of taking at least one management training course each year. One of the most useful courses was *Principles of Time Management*. That was twenty-five years ago, but I still try to practice many of the things I learned. My life experiences have reinforced their importance.

Most of us have known people who seem to always have plenty of time. They don't seem to rush, their work always appears caught up, their desks are uncluttered, and they are always on time. Many such people have just as busy lives as we do, but they never seem to show stress. I found that they are the ones who make effective use of their time. They are getting their most important tasks done on time by keeping their "eye on the donut."

Efficiency experts have identified a common human behavior they call the *Pareto Time Principle*. It states that average business workers spend eighty percent of their available time on trivial tasks that produce only twenty percent of their output. This means they spend only twenty percent of their time on important tasks that produce eighty percent of their production.

Stop and think for a minute. If we could focus one hundred percent (instead of the usual twenty percent) of our time on the vital situations or problems that produce eighty percent of the

Pa's Pearl's

results, our production would be four hundred percent of what the average worker might produce! This is where my "Donut Rule" comes into play. If we keep our eye on the donut—our real goal—we can avoid a lot of wasted time that brings us no appreciable return.

In reflecting on my own life's accomplishments, I can recall too many instances where I didn't make the most effective use of my time. Early in my career, I was one of ten chosen to receive six months of leadership training in Washington, DC. We attended various training courses and were expected to work on a variety of special projects that required written completion reports.

I was able to do a good job on several important projects, but I always regretted not using the opportunity to work with one or more of the important congressmen or senators of that day. As trainees, we had special access to work with them or their staffs on any of a number of important issues. Such experience would have provided valuable congressional contacts and experience that could have helped me during the rest of my career. I worked instead on several pet projects that were neither important nor productive. A golden opportunity forever lost.

In applying the Donut Rule to my life, it

dawned on me that one of my own vital tasks was pleasing my boss. Many people don't realize this may be the single, most important thing they can do for their career. Almost everybody has pet projects that accomplish nothing towards pleasing their boss or making him look good. They can be the "hole" instead of the "donut."

One would think this principle should be obvious to everyone. On the contrary, many people don't seem to really understand it. As a District Manager, I found that only a few of my Refuge Managers always had their reports completed on time, finished important tasks quickly, were prepared for my visits, and responded promptly to my requests. They were the effective managers who got the best performance evaluations and were promoted into more responsible jobs to become future leaders in our agency.

I routinely interviewed every refuge employee when I was doing inspections in my district. I occasionally found individuals who had become openly antagonistic and hostile towards their Refuge Manager. I tried to show them why pleasing their boss, even if they hated him, was in their own best interest. Though personalities might clash, it's always more effective to find a way for working with difficult superiors rather

Pa's Pearl's

than fighting them. They are, after all, the ones who rate our performance and hold a key to our advancement.

As I matured in my job and observed differences between employees who worked for me, I learned to refine my own performance behavior. I tried to always make my boss's slightest request one of the *vital* tasks that I gave highest priority. Even though I had other work I needed to finish, I tried to always respond to his needs first. Some might view this as currying favor, but it is actually a very sound and effective principle of both business and human relations management.

The *Pareto Time Principle* can be applied to almost any planning you might be doing—plans for the day, the month, or your lifetime. Take time to write a list of all the things you would like to accomplish and the steps needed to get them done. Group them into three categories: (a) vital tasks that must be done first; (b) important ones that can be temporarily deferred; and (c) nice-to-do tasks that can be put off indefinitely.

When you have decided these priorities, you will have a guide for getting the most accomplished during the time you have available. If you faithfully work toward getting your most important goals done first, your production should sharply increase and your stress level should subside. You will be keeping ", , , *your eye upon the donut* . . . ."

Lesson 11. Use It or Lose It (and Don't Abuse It)

It was the first track meet our small town high school had ever entered. I had trained for the high jump, broad jump, and two of the dashes. I was a bit dismayed when our coach came to me with a surprise request. He wanted me to do the mile run!

No one on our track team had trained for running the mile. I didn't even know if I could do it. Coach Bell coaxed me: "It doesn't matter how you do in this run, we just need somebody to enter and be part of the competition." Reluctantly, I agreed.

When the race started, I tried to keep up with the others. I was not a front-runner, but I was not the last either. When I finished the four laps around our quarter-mile cinder track, the coach had timed me at six minutes and ten seconds. Not a great time by any means, but certainly not bad for an unpracticed first try.

From that day on I started training for the mile run. I ran from my home on unpaved rural roads, sometimes as far as my friend's home about four miles away. I trained in heavy work boots and switched to light basketball shoes for the track meets.

With my serious training efforts, I began placing in the competition. The next year when I was a senior, I easily won first place at several meets, including the big invitational track meet that was the final event of the year. I set a Conference record of five minutes and five seconds that stood for several years.

After high school, almost twenty years passed before I returned to my running. That was thirty-seven years ago, and running has been a regular part of my life ever since. I have entered many different competitions, but my best time was never better than six minutes. Today I consider myself in excellent condition, but my ten-minute-mile is far from the six minutes it took for my first try.

My point in relating all this is to show just how fit a young teenager can be by nature, with no special training. When we are young, most of us have the natural gift of good physical fitness. You can see this in young kids who chase each other endlessly and never seem to be out of breath. I consider this fitness gift one of the most precious things any person ever has. It is something to be cherished, guarded, and nourished.

Good health and physical fitness can easily be squandered and lost. Once lost, they might never be regained. During my college years and for several years thereafter I squandered some of my health and fitness. I took up smoking for thirteen years and quit only after the Surgeon General issued his warning about its dangers. I didn't have any regular exercise program other than walking everywhere I went on campus. Except for basic training during my army days, I had no regular exercise regimen during the twenty years that followed high school, and my physical condition declined. Exercise wasn't stylish in those days, and we never saw anyone running, jogging, or even walking just for fitness. I never heard of a gym where average people went for strength training. I thought gyms were places where aspiring boxers went to train with sparring partners.

When I quit smoking and began running again, I started to realize how important such exercise was. Not only did I feel better, but I was also protecting my health, my longevity, and my very quality of life. Once you have gone through the pains of conditioning yourself for vigorous exercise and you experience the benefits of fitness, you don't want to ever lose that. Keeping your fitness and good health becomes one of the most important priorities of your life.

Friends who see me running often wonder how I am able to do it at my age. Some of them complain about bad knees that prevent them from running, or even walking any distance. I believe my knees have remained strong and healthy because I have kept them in condition with regular, vigorous running and walking. At eighteen to twenty miles a week, I run or walk more than a thousand miles each year just for exercise, over and beyond the incidental walking I do for other activities. Running has helped control my weight, and that is another factor that can cause knees to fail. My heart is healthy and strong, and I have the slow pulse typical for runners.

After retirement I began hearing and reading about newly discovered benefits of weight training. A neighbor who played professional football convinced me to join him at a nearby gym, and I added regular gym workouts to my fitness program. My chest measurements increased two inches and I lost two inches from my waist. I don't have backaches anymore. My good cholesterol (HDL) stays well above the desired level.

Looking back at my life, I realize more than ever how important it was to protect my body. I frequently see people my age or even younger who can hardly walk at all much less walk around the block. I think it's a tragedy when they have let that happen. The old maxim, *"Use it or lose it,"* is really true. Unlike our automobiles or other machines that wear out with frequent use, our bodies get stronger and extend their longevity with more frequent and continuous use. When you think of how important mobility is to quality of life, how can anyone just watch his or her physical fitness slip away?

Guarding our health is equally important as maintaining physical fitness. Smoking, obesity, or use of recreational drugs can all squander our health. So can the sedentary habits of "couch potatoes" who avoid exercise and risk obesity by sitting at computers or televisions during *all* their spare time. Smoking and obesity increase the chances of diabetes, cancer, hypertension, heart disease, or other problems. Chronic backaches can come from weak and lazy back and abdominal muscles. The effects of any one of these conditions can be devastating and very difficult to reverse. They can certainly ruin your quality of life.

If you've ever been around people who suffer severe health or fitness problems, you probably know how miserable it has made their lives. Besides the pain they might be suffering, they can also have the inconvenience of frequent doctor and hospital visits, the expense and bother of taking multiple prescription drugs, the loss of mobility, or the unwelcome need for someone else to care for them. Their quality of life can be vastly diminished and perhaps never recovered.

Please do not take all this as me bragging about my good physical condition. I consider that a blessing. Instead, I am trying to tell you about one of the most important values I have acquired during my lifetime. I hope my experiences can convince you to make your own commitment to physical fitness and a healthy lifestyle.

Start a regular exercise program early in your life and never give it up. If it becomes a habit—your way of life—you will never have to force yourself to do it. Take care of your body with good health habits and it will take care of you. Even a small commitment of time each day can pay big dividends for the rest of your life. Isn't it worth your time to protect such a precious gift?

Lesson 12: Mind Your Money

One of the toughest things we have to learn in life is good money management. This knowledge doesn't come naturally, and it's not often something we are taught in school. My mother *had* to stretch our family income, so I learned some of the basics from her. I had a lot more to figure out through my own experience.

Good money management boils down to one thing: making sure your income covers your spending. If you spend more than you make, you are going in debt, and that is definitely not good. It's really such a simple equation that it seems impossible for so many people to become victims of poor money management. Yet many do, mostly because they confuse their wants with their needs.

Many of today's young people never had to worry about their spending. Mom and Dad always provided the necessities of life—home, food, clothing, entertainment, an allowance, and maybe even a credit card. If they worked to earn their own money, they usually spent it any way they liked, mostly for non-essential luxuries. But starting out on their own they are suddenly faced with having to pay for everything they need.

John C. Oberheu

Not having rich parents, I knew about being frugal, but with my modest income I also needed to know about money management. I learned from my friends, through reading, and from my own trial and error. Today I want to pass on a few tricks that worked well for me.

Make a Budget. This is the first and most important thing any person should do to stay out of financial trouble. Begin by making a list of all regularly recurring monthly expenses, and show the amount you usually spend on each. Use categories such as: groceries, mortgage (or rent), insurance, utilities, telephone, credit card(s), savings, church, charities, and entertainment. Make a large miscellaneous category for things like clothes, doctors, dentists, auto repair, and similar monthly expenses that are irregular and may vary a lot. Add up the total costs and you will know just how far your paycheck must reach.

Track Your Spending. Keeping track of your income is easy. Everybody watches the numbers they see on their paycheck, and most people can tell you exactly how much they earn. The problems start when they have to make that paycheck cover their spending. To make your budget work, you must *know* where your paycheck is going. One way to find out is by keeping receipts for all your purchases and using them to make a monthly summary. Sort receipts by category, putting them in separate piles that can be added up to get category totals. Make a blank chart that lists all the budget categories you have chosen, or you can buy budget ledgers at an office supply store. Then keep a record of monthly totals for each category.

After five or six months you will have a good idea of where your money is going. You may find you want to adjust your budget targets for some categories. Soon you will begin to feel the satisfaction of knowing you are on sound financial footing.

Make Income Cover Essentials. Surviving on your own income can become difficult and scary. If you are not wealthy you will have to think in terms of priorities. Necessary things like food, clothing and lodging must come first. Quite often your income will not cover all you *think* you need, even for these basics.

Not to worry. There are many ways you can adjust your spending to help bring things into balance. My Lesson 4 on the art of being frugal makes numerous suggestions that can trim expenses. Practicing careful thrift can stretch your paycheck to cover more than you might at first think.

Begin by trimming things you don't really

need. Force yourself to be realistic. Even after doing this, you can still expect unplanned major expenses. Your car may need new tires, you might receive big insurance bill, or you have to see a dentist and he wants to put a $1,200 crown in your mouth. Then you have no choice but to operate on credit. The bill gets paid, but you have a new expense that your monthly paycheck must cover—the credit card payment. To avoid going backward into more debt, you must either increase your income or make another cut in other expenses.

Start a Savings Account. Unplanned major expenses, such as auto repair, dental work, or storm damage repair, can be difficult to manage. You might face large annual payments for homeowner insurance, auto insurance, termite control, or property tax. Some months your utility bill might exceed your budget because of unusual heating or cooling costs, or groceries may exceed your budget when you have houseguests for an extended period.

You can plan for such expenses by having a separate savings account to be used for paying them. Never try to keep savings in your checking account where they can "evaporate" through routine expenses. Add a "Savings" category to your budget, and each month, transfer a planned amount (at least ten percent of your income is a

Pa's Pearl's

good goal) into this account. When emergencies arise, you will be prepared. Savings that build in this account can also serve you well when you need a down payment for your first home.

Avoid the Debt Monster. The worst pitfall of good money management is debt. It is very easy to go into debt, but can be very difficult to climb out. Credit cards make it easy to buy things you can't really afford as well as paying for essentials like tires and dentist bills. You don't have to fork over actual cash, just a plastic credit card. The payments are stretched out, and it seems like an easy way to extend your budget. Wrong!

Credit card charges can become a trap. They might seem like a small addition to your monthly expenses, but if you examine each monthly statement you will find that you are paying a high interest rate for use of the lender's money. Most credit cards charge interest of twelve to twenty percent, and some will charge as high as twenty-five percent!

Every monthly credit card statement shows a finance charge that represents the interest due. Look at these finance charges as your enemy. *Interest buys you nothing!* It merely pays lenders for use of their money. At the end of the year when you see your annual statement showing how much interest you've paid, doesn't it make you kind of sick?

Watch the Easy Credit Trap. A second pitfall of good money management is easy credit. Suppose your first credit card is nearly maxed out, but there is a store or another credit card company offering new credit. Maybe you go ahead and buy that new fridge that you really need on the Sears "easy credit plan." Now you have two monthly credit card payments, and even more of your income goes to pay *interest that buys you nothing*.

Surprisingly, you find that your credit is still good, and other companies keep offering credit cards. If they are willing to give you credit, surely that means they know you can pay for it, right? Wrong!

You buy something else you think you really need, and even more of your income is going for interest. If you make only the minimum payments on each, the credit card folks are real happy. They continue to receive a high rate of return for their money, but your debt will be going down very slowly and your payments will continue for much longer. I have known people who were paying as many as six or more monthly credit card bills. They had trouble paying for basic groceries and rent.

"Consolidate your debt into one easy monthly payment," says the TV commercial. This seems

Pa's Pearl's

very sensible, and you do it. You get rid of several high-interest credit card bills and have only one monthly payment at a lower interest rate. This gives you more slack in your monthly expenses, you relax your control on spending and maybe even add to your debt. After six months at the low-interest starter rate, the standard rate kicks in. Your interest and payments go up, and you are spending even more of your income on *interest that buys you nothing.*

Don't Risk Your Dream. The next time you have trouble paying for groceries you may encounter the third pitfall—equity loans. You see another TV commercial: "Pay off your credit card debt," it coaxes. "Get a long-term, low-interest, equity loan on your home."

Your equity is the difference between the appraisal value of your home and the amount you still owe on your mortgage. You know your home has gone up in value, and a finance company will give you a long-term loan at a lower interest rate than your credit card account. They use your equity value as security for the money they lend you. "Might as well make use of that equity when I need it," you rationalize. "I have a long time to pay off my home."

This loan may have a lower interest rate than the credit card companies, but you will pay a financing fee up front and usually a higher interest rate than you are paying on your first mortgage. You will no longer have the equity you built up on your home, which was the main reason you wanted to buy a home and quit renting. Worse, you will owe more debt on your home, and be even farther from your retirement goal of having a debt-free home.

At this point you must sharply curb your spending or you will soon be in serious trouble. Now if your paycheck won't stretch, you will have only one option left: bankruptcy. Lenders will foreclose on your valuable property items to recover some of their losses on your unpaid debts. Your credit rating will be ruined for at least five years, and this will mean that interest rates will be higher on any loan you might find. You will have to start all over trying to make your paycheck cover your real needs.

I have painted a "worse-case scenario" that is not at all uncommon today. The number of personal bankruptcies in the nation reached an all time high in 2005. Hopefully, it will never happen to you, but don't forget, debt is a monster that can devour you if you fall into its clutches.

Cut Banking Costs. Also needed for minding your money is a bank account that works for you. Some banks make monthly service charges and require costly ATM fees. Banks offer different kinds of accounts, and some will require a fee for every check you write. Depending on how many you write, this can be a big cost. Some banks may charge exorbitant fees if you have a check bounce or have to cancel one. You will find, however, that different banks have very different policies on such things.

It's smart to shop around at different banks to find the best deal for your accounts. Don't stay with a bank that charges you a monthly service fee regardless of how much is in the account. Some banks will waive monthly service charges if you keep your checking account above a certain minimum. A few will even pay a low interest rate on the average monthly balance in your checking account as well as for your savings account.

Don't settle for anything less than an interest-bearing checking account. You may have to keep a certain minimum balance to avoid service fees and draw interest, but this is a very wise thing to do. Keep a close eye on your running bank balance to avoid any penalties. That minimum balance you maintain can also provide a buffer if you ever make a mistake on your balance and bring it below the minimum. If that happens, you might have to pay a service fee for the month, but you might avoid the more costly mistake of overdrawing the account.

Put Your Money to Work. Be sure to protect your savings in a separate account. Saving accounts always pay more interest, and interest added to your account is like another paycheck. Ask your bank about linking your savings account with your checking account so that you will not be charged a penalty for mistakenly overdrawing the checking account. If you overdraw, the overdraft will be taken from savings.

Always deposit unexpected or bonus income into the savings account. Large income tax refunds, an inheritance check, a scholarship check, a large rebate or refund on something you have purchased—all should go into savings rather than checking account where it might disappear for living expenses. Try to defer the instant gratification you might want from a new car, boat, or TV.

Take pride in your savings account and enjoy watching it grow. When it gets large enough that you are ready to invest some of it where it can bring an even better return, it will be time to get some sound and trustworthy advice. Find a person you can trust who is experienced in the many investment options and the risks of each. Don't make a dumb mistake by following some hot tip or letting a con man talk you into putting hard-earned savings into a "sure-fire" investment scam.

Make Credit Cards Work for You. I have already covered the pitfalls that await you with credit card accounts, but I want to add some thoughts on how a credit card can help you manage your finances. It took me years to learn this, but I have found it very useful and convenient.

Never keep a credit card that charges an annual fee because there are so many that do not. Choose one national credit card that you like the best, and charge everything you can to that account. Pay for groceries, K-Mart purchases, gas, car repair, drugs, doctors, dentists, video rentals, airline tickets, restaurants, motels—everything. This may seem to conflict with what I have been telling you about reducing and getting rid of your debt, but this will not change that advice. Just make sure everything that you charge is within your budget.

At the end of the month you will receive a large credit card bill. It may scare you at first, but the money you would have paid out for the same items will be resting in your checking account and drawing interest. Pay the bill with one big check, *and be sure to send it in on time.* You will pay no interest. You will not have to write a check every time you buy something, or make frequent cash withdrawals from your checking account. You can carry less cash on your person and avoid dealing with pennies and small change. You will build a good credit rating, and after several months your credit limit will be raised. You will get a monthly report of your expenditures by category, and if you have the right credit card, you can even get cash back on what you have spent. I have received cash-back refunds of over $200 a year from my Discover Card.

Don't Forget Retirement. I addressed the need for you to save for retirement in my Lesson 4, but I have a few more reminders. If you are not having automatic monthly payments put into retirement instruments like IRAs or a 401 plan, you should try to do so by using any available surplus from your cash reserves. Investments in such instruments can grow faster because they are not taxed until they are withdrawn.

When you buy a home, treat the equity you are building as a retirement savings. You have merely to look at your monthly budget to see that housing is your biggest monthly expense. If you have just bought your home, you know that the biggest portion of each month's house payment is, by far, to pay *interest that buys you nothing*. It's important to keep in mind that the more your loan is reduced, the greater will be the portion of your payment that reduces your debt and builds your

Pa's Pearl's

equity. A debt-free home when you are retired is as good as a monthly check for the amount you would otherwise have to spend for housing. Everyone's income is reduced at retirement, and owning a debt-free home will give you much peace of mind.

Manage Your Mortgage. Buying a home is probably the biggest purchase you will ever make. Learning how a home mortgage works is well worth your time.

A thirty-year loan of $100,000 at seven percent interest will require a monthly payment of $665.30. Your first payment will take $583.33 for the first month's interest and will reduce your debt by only $81.97. Almost eighty-eight percent of the payment will be for interest! At the end of one year, you will have paid $6,968 in interest and reduced your debt by only $1,016. For every $1.00 of debt reduction, you will have paid $6.85 for interest.

You can learn more interesting facts by studying an amortization table. For example, if you make a double payment during the first month of your mortgage, you can cut twelve monthly payments off the life of your mortgage. Keep this principle in mind if you have money to invest. Extra mortgage payments go entirely toward debt reduction and can greatly shorten the life of your mortgage, especially in its early years.

If you pay no more than your monthly payment of $665.30 each month, the portion of each payment that goes for interest will exceed the amount that reduces your debt until the end of the twentieth year. At that time, you will have paid off only $43,364 and will have paid $117,639 in interest, or $2.71 in interest for every $1.00 of debt. If you never make more than your regular monthly payment until it is paid off, you will have paid $139,509 in interest for your loan of $100,000! Some of these costs might, of course, be offset if you use them for income tax deductions.

I am not giving these facts to warn you away from going into debt to buy a home, but rather to show you how much interest is paid with a large, long-term loan. A home mortgage is a necessary evil to move you towards eventual home ownership, but the interest you will pay is an important consideration.

Avoiding interest payments can be as good (or even better) than receiving interest payments. There was a time during the late 1980's when Lucy and I were paying twelve percent interest on our home mortgage. Banks were paying about six percent interest, and the best money markets were paying eight percent. Instead of putting our extra income into savings or other investments, we chose to pay down that mortgage. We paid off our home years ahead of schedule, and saved thousands of dollars in interest.

This bald-headed old-timer's advice on money management has become much longer than I like, but there was a lot to cover. I have worked to make it understandable, and I have tried to include every important financial management trick I learned since I started paying my own bills. That was a long, long time ago, and I wish I could have had all this knowledge back then. I hope these thoughts will help you plan your own fiscal strategies to *"mind your money."*

Lesson 13: Be A Role Model

"Remember second grade?" read the subject line of an email from an unknown address. When my son-in-law opened it, the message warmed his heart:

"Hi David! This is a flash from the past. I want you to know that you are remembered still for a very big kindness you did for me in second grade. I have used it as an example of 'doing unto others' for my kids."

David had left his name and email address at ClassMates.com, an Internet website for finding old friends. His first response was from a girl he hadn't seen in twenty-five years.

"One day the teacher would not let me go to the bathroom because it was only ten minutes till recess," the message went on. "I couldn't hold it anymore and wet all over the floor. You sat behind me and had to move your feet, but you never said a word to anyone. When recess started, you stayed behind with me to help clean it up. I never got teased or anything. That always meant a lot to me, and I don't think I ever told you. I can only assume that you are still a man of character. Thanks, David!"

It's a bit of a stretch to think of a second grader as a role model, but this true story shows that it can actually happen. If you pause to really think about it, there are role models throughout our entire life. Our parents are usually the first and most influential, the ones who teach us our basic value system. But there are friends we admire and many others who also help mold our interests, likes and dislikes.

Teachers are important role models. Those who earn our special respect and admiration help form our value system and outlook on life. I remember especially my high school English teacher who taught me writing and grammar skills. She also directed the school chorus and taught me music principles that have enriched my life. My major professor in college inspired me to learn a profession that brought me a lifetime of fulfillment and satisfaction.

The farmer who hired me during my high school summers was a man I greatly admired. He taught me to do most all the tasks required on a large and busy farm, and we shared the simple joys of hard work and the hearty meals his wife fed us. He instilled in me a reverence for the land, a respect for good stewardship of the soil, and his special love for the farm animals. I learned care and maintenance for expensive tools and machinery—practices I still use today.

Even strangers can be role models. I'll never

Pa's Pearl's

forget the man standing behind me when I was buying a ticket for the movie theater. It was the first time the ticket lady asked me how old I was. I had been passing for the kid's admission of twelve cents, and that's all the money I had. When I truthfully answered that I was twelve, she had to require the full admission price of thirty-seven cents. I was turning away in tears when the man behind me paid the difference. His was a small act of kindness for a kid he didn't even know. It deeply impressed me, however, and I never forgot it. I've had opportunity to pass on his kindness several times in my life, and it always makes me feel good.

My college lab partner in Comparative Anatomy was a World War II vet who was eight years my senior. Jack had been an Army officer who had special leadership training. He became my mentor in teaching me independence and self-reliance. He was my coach when I started my first permanent job. We followed almost parallel careers, and he became my frequent consultant and confidant.

One day Jack and I were walking to lunch on an Atlanta street. A poorly dressed homeless man approached and asked for money to get something to eat. Brushing him off as a wino who would spend anything we gave him on booze, we ignored him and crossed the street. As we reached the other side, Jack commented: "You know, that man might *really* be hungry!" All at once I felt guilt for not sensing that man's need and responding in a way that could have helped him.

To this day, I remember that feeling every time someone asks me for food money. I am blessed never to have been really hungry, but I can never again feel comfortable in ignoring someone's plea for food. I would rather help an undeserving person than pass someone in such desperate need that pride was overcome to resort to begging. This is a lifetime value I learned from my friend Jack, one of my important role models.

When we seize an opportunity to help someone, the ripple effects of our action can carry farther than we ever dreamed. David responded to his classmate as he did because he felt it was the right thing to do—a value learned from his parents. His consideration and courtesy saved her from unnecessary embarrassment and the almost certain ridicule of her classmates. It meant so much to her that she used his example to teach her own children, and they will also remember his kindness.

This remarkable flashback to a second grade incident from a quarter century ago ought to give us pause. We do not often hear about long-term effects of simple kindnesses we show to others, but here is evidence of the impact they can have. In like manner, thoughtless or hateful acts can inflict lasting hurt and injured feelings that are never forgotten.

Our children and others around us can learn either good or evil from our behavior. Kind actions can leave a legacy like David's: a warm and lasting memory of friendship and courtesy; a life lesson to be passed to future generations.

Always remember, people are watching. *You can be a role model—for good behavior . . . or for bad!*

Epilogue
To my granddaughters

Compiling and publishing these essays has been a long and arduous task. I tried to include every worthwhile lesson from my life that I thought might be useful to you. I did not include sexual or religious topics because you have better teachers than me to convey those lessons. Although I still think of other incidents or issues which were my teachers, I am now convinced that all the most important lessons of my life are here. When you finish reading this book, you should have a pretty good idea of how your Grandpa thinks.

I wish for you a long life filled with the blessings of happiness, prosperity, and good health. *And may you grow smart before you grow old!*

With all my love,

Pa